by
## Scott Jung

**Marty n' Luther's Comic Catechism**
Written and illustrated by Scott Jung

Scriptures quoted from *The Holy Bible, New Century Version*®, copyright © 1987, 1988, 1991 by Word Publishing, a division of Thomas Nelson, Inc. Used by permission.

ISBN 978-1-4303-1533-9

Printed by www.lulu.com

# Contents

WELCOME TO

## Marty n' Luther's Comic Catechism

FOR MANY, THE BiBLE iS AN iNTiMiDATiNG BOOK.

IT iS SO BiG AND CONTAiNS STORiES THAT HAPPENED THOUSANDS OF YEARS AGO.

BUT THE MESSAGE OF THE BiBLE iS ACTUALLY VERY SiMPLE.

IN 1529, A CHRiSTiAN MAN BY THE NAME OF MARTiN LUTHER WROTE A SiMPLE BOOK TO HELP PARENTS EXPLAiN TO THEiR CHiLDREN WHAT THE BiBLE TEACHES.

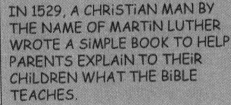

HE SUMMARiZED THE WHOLE BiBLE BY EXPLAiNiNG SiX DiFFERENT PARTS.

1. GOD'S TEN COMMANDS
2. THE APOSTLES' BELIEFS
3. JESUS' PRAYER
4. BAPTISM
5. CONFESSION & FORGIVENESS
6. JESUS' SUPPER

# God's Ten Commands

GOD'S TEN COMMANDS TELL YOU WHAT GOD EXPECTS OF YOU. HIS TEN COMMANDS CAN BE DIVIDED IN TWO PARTS. THE FIRST THREE COMMANDS DESCRIBE YOUR RELATIONSHIP WITH GOD. THE LAST SEVEN COMMANDS DESCRIBE YOUR RELATIONSHIP WITH OTHERS.

1. You will not have other gods.
2. You will not misuse God's name.
3. You will remember the Sabbath day by keeping it special.
4. You will honor your parents.
5. You will not kill.
6. You will not be sexually unfaithful.
7. You will not steal.
8. You will not lie about your neighbor.
9. You will not desire your neighbor's house.
10. You will not desire your neighbor's spouse, workers, animals, or anything that belongs to your neighbor.

## God's Second Command
"You will not misuse God's name."

# God's Sixth Command

"You will not be sexually unfaithful."

DO YOU GET iT?

OUT OF RESPECT AND LOVE FOR GOD, YOU SHOULD BE SEXUALLY PURE...

... iN WHAT YOU SAY...

... AND WHAT YOU DO.

HUSBANDS AND WiVES SHOULD LOVE AND RESPECT EACH OTHER.

# God's Seventh Command
"You will not steal."

DO YOU GET iT?

OUT OF RESPECT AND LOVE FOR GOD, YOU SHOULD NOT TAKE WHAT BELONGS TO OTHERS OR CHEAT THEM OUT OF iT.

YOU SHOULD HELP THEM iMPROVE AND PROTECT WHAT BELONGS TO THEM.

## God's Ninth Command

"You will not desire your neighbor's house."

DO YOU GET iT?
OUT OF RESPECT AND LOVE FOR GOD, YOU SHOULD NOT
MAKE PLANS iN YOUR HEART TO TAKE WHAT BELONGS
TO OTHERS. YOU SHOULD THANK GOD FOR THE THiNGS
HE GiVES YOU, AND HELP OTHERS HOLD ONTO WHAT GOD
HAS GiVEN THEM.

## God's Tenth Command

"You will not desire your neighbor's spouse,
workers, animals, or anything that belongs
to your neighbor."

DO YOU GET iT?
OUT OF RESPECT AND LOVE FOR GOD,
YOU SHOULD NOT MAKE PLANS iN YOUR
HEART TO TAKE OTHERS' RELATiONSHiPS
(SUCH AS FRiENDS, SPOUSES, WORKERS)
AWAY FROM THEM OR TURN OTHERS
AGAiNST THEM.
YOU SHOULD ENCOURAGE THEM
TO CONTiNUE iN THEiR
GOD-GiVEN ROLE.

13

# Conclusion to God's Ten Commands

"You must not worship or serve any idol, because I, the Lord your God, am a jealous God. If you hate me, I will punish your children, and even your grandchildren and great-grandchildren. But I show kindness to thousands who love me and obey my commands." Exodus 20:5-6

DO YOU GET iT? GOD THREATENS TO PUNiSH ALL WHO DiSOBEY HiS COMMANDS.

YOU SHOULD FEAR HiS PUNiSHMENT AND OBEY HiM.

BUT GOD ALSO PROMiSES TO REWARD ALL WHO OBEY HiS COMMANDS.

YOU SHOULD LOVE AND TRUST HiM, AND CHEERFULLY DO WHAT HE COMMANDS.

# The Apostles' Beliefs

GOD'S TEN COMMANDS TELL YOU THAT EVERYONE IS SINFUL AND NEEDS GOD'S RESCUE. THE APOSTLES' BELIEFS TELL YOU HOW THE THREE-IN-ONE GOD (FATHER, SON, AND HOLY SPIRIT) WORKED TO CREATE YOU, RESCUE YOU FROM YOUR SINFULNESS, AND MAKE YOU CLEAN IN HIS EYES.

I believe in God the all-powerful Father, maker of all that is seen and unseen.

I believe in Jesus the Messiah, God's only Son, our Master. He was conceived by the Holy Spirit. He was born to Mary, a virgin. Pontius Pilate made him suffer. He was crucified, put to death, and buried. He went down to hell. Three days later he rose from the dead. He went up to heaven and rules with God the all-powerful Father. He will return one day to judge everyone, alive and dead.

I believe in the Holy Spirit, the one Christian church made up of saints, the forgiveness of sins, the bodily resurrection, and eternal life in heaven.

19

## God the Son

"I believe in Jesus the Messiah, God's only Son, our Master. He was conceived by the Holy Spirit. He was born to Mary, a virgin. Pontius Pilate made him suffer. He was crucified, put to death, and buried. He went down to hell. Three days later he rose from the dead. He went up to heaven and rules with God the all-powerful Father. He will return one day to judge everyone, alive and dead."

22

## God the Holy Spirit

"I believe in the Holy Spirit, the one Christian church made up of saints, the forgiveness of sins, the bodily resurrection, and eternal life in heaven.

# Jesus' Prayer

PRAYER IS TALKING WITH GOD. JESUS TAUGHT HIS FOLLOWERS HOW TO PRAY. JESUS' PRAYER IS MADE UP OF SEVEN REQUESTS THAT GOD PROMISES TO ANSWER.

Our Father in heaven,
Please keep your name holy.
Please let your kingdom come.
Please let your will be done on earth, just like heaven.
Please give daily bread to us.
Please forgive our sins as we now forgive the sins others have done to us.
Please keep us away from temptation.
Please save us from evil.
Because it is your kingdom, your power, and your glory, forever and ever. Amen.

DO YOU GET iT?

GOD'S NAME iS HOLY WHETHER YOU ASK iT TO BE OR NOT.

IN THiS REQUEST, YOU ARE ASKiNG GOD TO HELP YOU CORRECTLY TEACH AND HEAR HiS WORD, AND TO DO WHAT iT SAYS.

iS THE SAVIOR

iS NOT THE SAVIOR

BUDDHISM

ISLAMIC

JUDAISM

YOU ARE ALSO ASKiNG FOR GOD'S PROTECTiON FROM THOSE WHO TEACH LiES ABOUT GOD'S WORD AND DON'T DO WHAT iT SAYS.

## The Second Request

"Please let your kingdom come."

DO YOU GET iT?

GOD'S KiNGDOM WiLL COME WHETHER YOU ASK FOR iT OR NOT.

IN THiS REQUEST, YOU ARE ASKiNG THAT GOD, BY HiS GRACE, WiLL GiVE YOU HiS HOLY SPiRiT...

... SO THAT YOU MAY BELiEVE HiS WORD ...

... AND LiVE A GOD-PLEASiNG LiFE ...

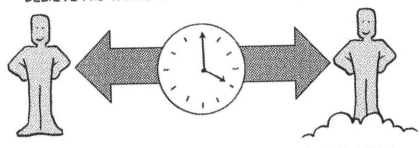

... BOTH NOW ON EARTH AND EVENTUALLY iN HEAVEN.

# The Third Request

"Please let your will be done on earth just like in heaven."

DO YOU GET iT?

GOD'S WiLL iS DONE WHETHER YOU ASK FOR iT OR NOT.

IN THiS REQUEST, YOU ARE ASKiNG GOD TO STOP THE REBELLiOUS PLANS OF SATAN, THE WORLD, AND YOUR SiNFUL NATURE.

YOU ARE ASKiNG GOD TO CONTiNUE HiS PLAN OF HELPiNG YOU KEEP HiS NAME HOLY, SENDiNG YOU HiS HOLY SPiRiT, AND KEEPiNG YOUR FAiTH STRONG UNTiL DEATH.

# The Sixth Request
"Please keep us away from temptation."

# The Sacraments

A SACRAMENT IS A SPECIAL ACT COMMANDED BY
JESUS. A SACRAMENT IS SOMETHING VISUAL THAT
CONNECTS US TO GOD'S FORGIVENESS OFFERED
THROUGH JESUS. THE TWO SACRAMENTS ARE BAPTISM
AND JESUS' SUPPER.

The Sacrament of Baptism

Confession and Forgiveness

The Sacrament of Jesus' Supper.

# The Sacrament of Baptism
## What is baptism?

BAPTISM IS NOT JUST ORDINARY WATER. IT IS WATER CONNECTED TO JESUS' COMMAND, AND CONNECTED TO GOD'S WORD.

"So go and make followers of all people in the world. Baptize them in the name of the Father and the Son and the Holy Spirit."
Matthew 28:19

# The Sacrament of Baptism
## How does baptism benefit me?

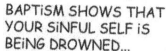

# The Sacrament of Baptism
## What does baptism with water show?

BAPTiSM SHOWS THAT YOUR SiNFUL SELF iS BEiNG DROWNED...

... AND A NEW YOU iS BEiNG RAiSED TO LiVE BEFORE GOD, WASHED CLEAN AND PURE.

"When we were baptized, we were buried with Christ and shared his death. So, just as Christ was raised from the dead by the wonderful power of the Father, we also can live a new life." Romans 6:4

# Confession and Forgiveness
## What is confession?

THERE ARE TWO PARTS TO CONFESSiON.

FiRST, YOU ADMiT THAT YOU ARE SiNFUL.

SECONDLY, YOU RECEiVE GOD'S ANNOUNCEMENT OF FORGiVENESS THROUGH YOUR PASTOR.

I'm sorry.

God forgives you.

## What sins should you confess?

BEFORE GOD, YOU SHOULD CONFESS THAT YOU ARE GUiLTY OF ALL SiNS, EVEN THOSE YOU DiD UNKNOWiNGLY.

BEFORE YOUR PASTOR, YOU SHOULD CONFESS ONLY THE SiNS YOU KNOW OF THAT ARE WEiGHiNG ON YOUR HEART.

# Confession and Forgiveness
How do you know what to confess?

THINK ABOUT YOUR LIFE ACCORDING TO GOD'S TEN COMMANDS.

ARE YOU A DAD, MOM, SON, DAUGHTER, HUSBAND, WIFE, STUDENT, OR WORKER?

HAVE YOU BEEN DISOBEDIENT, DECEITFUL, OR LAZY?

HAVE YOU BEEN ANGRY, RUDE, OR A TROUBLE-MAKER? HAVE YOU USED YOUR WORDS OR ACTIONS TO HURT SOMEONE?

HAVE YOU STOLEN ANYTHING, BEEN IRRESPONSIBLE, WASTEFUL, OR HURTFUL?

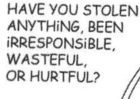

46

## Confession and Forgiveness
### What is the Office of the Keys?

GOD GAVE SPECIAL RESPONSIBILITY
TO THE CHURCH IN JOHN 20:22-23...

"After he said this, he breathed on them
and said, 'Receive the Holy Spirit. If you
forgive anyone his sins, they are forgiven.
If you don't forgive them, they are not
forgiven.'" John 20:22-23

ONE KEY LOCKS THE
DOOR OF FORGIVENESS
UNTIL THEY ARE SORRY
FOR THEIR SINS.

ONE KEY OPENS THE
DOOR OF FORGIVENESS
FOR THOSE WHO ARE
SORRY FOR THEIR SINS.

PASTORS ARE CALLED BY THE
CHURCH TO CARRY OUT THIS
RESPONSIBILITY AS IF JESUS
WAS DOING IT HIMSELF.

**47**

# The Sacrament of Jesus' Supper
## What is Jesus' Supper?

JESUS' SUPPER IS A SPECIAL MEAL CREATED BY JESUS. IN THE MEAL, JESUS OFFERS HIS TRUE BODY AND BLOOD WITH THE VISIBLE BREAD AND WINE.

THIS MEAL IS INTENDED FOR CHRISTIANS.

"On the night when the Lord Jesus was handed over to be killed, he took bread and gave thanks for it. Then he broke the bread and said, 'This is my body; it is for you. Do this to remember me.' In the same way, after they ate, Jesus took the cup. He said, 'Every one of you drink this. This is my blood which is the new agreement that God makes with his people. This blood is poured out for many to forgive their sins. When you drink this, do it to remember me.'"
1 Corinthians 11:23-25; Matthew 26:26-28; Mark 14:22-24; Luke 22:19-20

How does Jesus' Supper benefit you?

JESUS' SUPPER GiVES YOU
FORGiVENESS OF SiNS.

THE MEAL ALSO OFFERS YOU
LiFE AND SALVATiON, BECAUSE
THESE ARE DiRECTLY CONNECTED
TO THE FORGiVENESS OF SiNS.

How can eating and drinking do
such amazing things?

GOD'S WORDS, "GiVEN AND SHED
FOR YOU TO FORGiVE YOUR SiNS,"
ALONG WiTH THE PHYSiCAL
EATiNG AND DRiNKiNG, ARE
THE iMPORTANT THiNG.

IF YOU BELiEVE THESE WORDS,
YOU HAVE JUST WHAT THEY PROMiSE:
YOUR SiNS ARE FORGiVEN!

# Extras

Daily Prayers

Mealtime Prayers

Duties & Responsibilities

Luther's Emblem

# Daily Prayers

## Morning Prayer

*In the morning when you wake up,
make the sign of the cross and say...*

In the name of the Father and the Son and the Holy Spirit. Amen.

My Father in heaven, I thank you through Your Son Jesus for protecting me last night from all harm and danger. Please also protect me today from sin and evil. I want my entire life to please You. I place myself, my body and soul, and everything I have in Your hands. Let Your angels be with me, so that Satan has no control over me. Amen.

## Evening Prayer

*In the evening before you go to bed,
make the sign of the cross and say...*

In the name of the Father and the Son and the Holy Spirit. Amen.

My Father in heaven, I thank you through Your Son Jesus for protecting me today. Please forgive all the times I did the wrong thing and sinned against You. Please watch over me tonight. I place myself, my body and soul, and everything I have into Your hands. Let Your angels be with me, so that Satan has no control over me. Amen.

# Mealtime Prayers

## Before Eating

*Your family can sit down at the table honoring God by folding your hands and saying...*

"All living things look to you for food, and you give it to them at right time. You open your hand and satisfy all living things."
Psalm 145:15-16

*Then you can say Jesus' Prayer and this:*

Our Father in heaven, bless us and all these gifts we receive from your amazing goodness. We pray because of Jesus Christ our Lord. Amen.

## After Eating

*Your family can leave the table honoring God by folding your hands and saying...*

"Give thanks to the Lord because he is good. His love continues forever. He gives food to every living creature. He gives food to cattle and to the little birds that call. He does not enjoy the strength of a horse or the strength of a man. The Lord is pleased with those who respect him, with those who trust his love."
Psalm 136:1,25; 147:9-11

*Then you can say Jesus' Prayer and this:*

We thank you, Father in heaven, for all the good things you give us. We pray because of Jesus Christ our Lord, living and reigning with you and the Holy Spirit for all time. Amen.

# Duties and Responsibilities

## Pastors

"An elder must not give people a reason to criticize him, and he must have only one wife. He must be self-controlled, wise, respected by others, ready to welcome guests, and able to teach. He must not drink too much wine or like to fight, but rather be gentle and peaceable, not loving money. He must be a good family leader, having children who cooperate with full respect. (If someone does not know how to lead the family, how can that person take care of God's church?) But an elder must not be a new believer, or he might be too proud of himself and be judged guilty just as the devil was." 1 Timothy 3:2-6

*Also Titus 1:9*

## Congregation Members

"Now, brothers and sisters, we ask you to appreciate those who work hard among you, who lead you in the Lord and teach you. Respect them with a very special love because of the work they do. Live in peace with each other." 1 Thessalonians 5:12-13

*Also 1 Corinthians 9:14; Galatians 6:6-7; 1 Timothy 5:17-18; Hebrews 13:17*

# Duties and Responsibilities

## Government

"All of you must yield to the government rulers. No one rules unless God has given him the power to rule, and no one rules now without that power from God. So those who are against the government are really against what God has commanded. And they will bring punishment on themselves. Those who do right do not have to fear the rulers; only those who do wrong fear them. Do you want to be unafraid of the rulers? Then do what is right, and they will praise you. The ruler is God's servant to help you. But if you do wrong, then be afraid. He has the power to punish; he is God's servant to punish those who do wrong." Romans 13:1-4

## Citizens

"For the Lord's sake, yield to the people who have authority in this world: the king, who is the highest authority, and the leaders who are sent by him to punish those who do wrong and to praise those who do right." 1 Peter 2:13-14

"So you must yield to the government, not only because you might be punished, but because you know it is right. This is also why you pay taxes. Rulers are working for God and give their time to their work. Pay everyone, then, what you owe. If you owe any kind of tax, pay it. Show respect and honor to them all." Romans 13:5-7

"Jesus said to them, 'Give to Caesar the things that are Caesar's, and to God the things that are God's.'" Matthew 22:21

*Also 1 Timothy 2:1-3; Titus 3:1*

# Duties and Responsibilities

## Husbands

"Husbands, love your wives and be gentle with them."
Colossians 3:19

*Also 1 Peter 3:7*

## Wives

"Wives, yield to your husbands, as you do to the Lord."
Ephesians 5:22

*Also 1 Peter 3:5-6*

## Parents

"Fathers, do not make your children angry, but raise them with the training and teaching of the Lord." Ephesians 6:4

## Children

"Children, obey your parents as the Lord wants, because this is the right thing to do. The command says, 'Honor your father and mother.' This is the first command that has a promise with it—'Then everything will be well with you, and you will have a long life on the earth.'" Ephesians 6:1-3

# Duties and Responsibilities

## Workers

"Slaves, obey your masters here on earth with fear and respect and from a sincere heart, just as you obey Christ. You must do this not only while they are watching you, to please them. With all your heart you must do what God wants as people who are obeying Christ. Do your work with enthusiasm. Work as if you were serving the Lord, not as if you were serving only men and women. Remember that the Lord will give a reward to everyone, slave or free, for doing good." Ephesians 6:5-8

## Bosses

"Masters, in the same way, be good to your slaves. Do not threaten them. Remember that the One who is your Master and their Master is in heaven, and he treats everyone alike." Ephesians 6:9

## Youth

"In the same way, younger people should be willing to be under older people. And all of you should be very humble with each other. 'God is against the proud, but he gives grace to the humble.' Be humble under God's powerful hand so he will lift you up when the right time comes." 1 Peter 5:5-6

## Widows

"The true widow, who is all alone, puts her hope in God and continues to pray night and day for God's help. But the widow who uses her life to please herself is really dead while she is alive." 1 Timothy 5:5-6

## Youth

"The law says, 'You must not be guilty of adultery. You must not murder anyone. You must not steal. You must not want to take your neighbor's things.' All these commands and all others are really only one rule: 'Love your neighbor as you love yourself.'" Romans 13:9

# Luther's Emblem

**The Black Cross** reminds you that you are a sinner, and that Jesus died on the cross to suffer the punishment you deserved.

**The Red Heart** reminds you how much God loved you by sending Jesus to be your Savior. The color red also reminds you of the blood of Jesus to forgive your sins.

**The White Rose** reminds you that the Holy Spirit makes you clean and pure in God's eyes by giving you faith in Jesus and helping you live the way God wants.

**The Blue Background** reminds you of the joy you have because God gave you new life.

**The Gold Ring** reminds you of the promise of heaven, where you will always have joy and happiness with Jesus.

CPSIA information can be obtained
at www.ICGtesting.com
Printed in the USA
BVHW071417120620
581230BV00004B/201

9 781430 315339